CarlySimon

text   **Charles and Ann Morse**
illustrations   **Dick Brude**
design concept   **Mark Landkamer**

published by   **Creative Education**
Mankato, Minnesota

Published by Creative Educational Society, Inc.,
123 South Broad Street, Mankato, Minnesota 56001
Copyright © 1975 by Creative Educational Society, Inc. International
copyrights reserved in all countries.
No part of this book may be reproduced in any form without written permission
from the publisher. Printed in the United States.
Distributed by Childrens Press, 1224 West Van Buren Street, Chicago, Illinois 60607
Library of Congress Number: 74-14550   ISBN: 0-87191-393-3
Library of Congress Cataloging in Publication Data
Morse, Charles.   Carly Simon.
SUMMARY: A biography stressing the musical career of
composer-folk singer Carly Simon.
1. Simon, Carly—Juvenile lit. [1. Simon, Carly. 2. Singers, American]
I. Morse, Ann, joint author. II. Brude, Dick, illus. III. Title.
ML3930.S55M7   784'.092'4 [B] [92]   74-14550
ISBN 0-87191-393-3

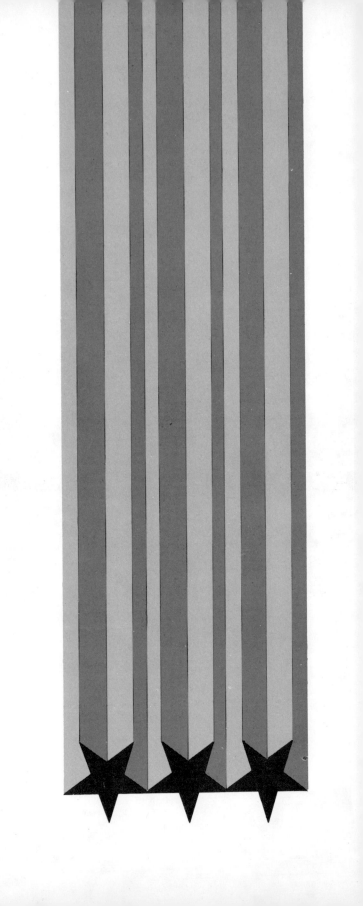

Embrace Me You Child

"Embrace me you child; you're a child of mine. I'm leaving everything I am to you . . ."

Heat steamed from the streets of New York that July 29, 1960. It was blistering hot, but the sun wasn't shining for 17-year-old Carly Simon. Her father had died that day.

From the time Richard Simon, co-founder of Simon and Schuster Publishing Company, had had his first heart attack some years before, Carly had lived in fear of his death. She would knock on wood 500 times a day and pray every night that she wouldn't lose her father. It was Carly's way of working magic to keep death away from her father.

Carly had feared his death so much that she would often move away from him when he was ill. By being near him, Carly feared that she, too, would die. These feelings bewildered Carly. After her father died, she covered up her feelings. But they were still there, lingering through the years.

Eleven years later Carly sat down with a book of blank pages and a pencil. She decided to write whatever came into her head.

The first line she wrote in that book had God whispering lullabies to her. Carly didn't know where those words came from, but somehow they ran on into the second line, "And Daddy next door whistled whiskey tunes." Each line went on to another line.

At the end of 2 verses, Carly knew something strange was happening. In the song her father is pictured as a frightening character. Carly had always been very fond of her father and was proud of his many achievements. Still she began to see that somewhere in her mind her father must have seemed terribly awesome to her.

The song was called "Embrace Me, You Child." Its

last verse continues the story:

"Then one night Daddy died and went to heaven,
And God came down to earth and slipped away. I
I pretended not to know I'd been abandoned. . . ."

In recent interviews Carly has said that she felt abandoned by her father and by God. She said, "Losing my father also meant losing my faith in God whom I had prayed to every night."

"Embrace Me, You Child" wasn't planned; it just happened. "It was as if I had somebody sitting there writing for me," Carly once said. It is a mysterious song and really doesn't need to be figured out. It's a song that reveals some of Carly Simon's mind.

Carly Simon is not just a folk singer with a pretty voice. She can sing in many different styles — folk, rock, country western, classical. But Carly's music should be described as the kind of rock that gets inside and pushes the listener to reach out. She pulls her songs out of her own experiences and gives them the feeling of real life.

The Best Thing

"How was I to know it was the best thing to come along for a long time"

Being the third of 4 children, Carly always considered herself a loser. "Having 2 older sisters gave me little sense of myself when I was growing up," Carly says.

Once when Carly was 4, a nurse came to their house to help with Peter, the youngest Simon who had just been born. Joanna, who was 10, greeted the nurse in a queenly manner. Then Lucy, 7, said hello in her angelic way. When it was Carly's turn, she thought, "What's left for me?" In order to be different, Carly jumped up on a coffee

Em-brace me you child, you're
child of mine.
ing ev 'ry-thing
I am to you.

table and did an imitation of Al Jolson. From then on she became the family clown. "It was the only way I could think of to get any attention," she has said.

Music always held the attention of the Simon family. Carly says that she was born into a family that had a way with tunes. "My mother sang 'Lullaby and Goodnight' until dawn, while my father played Chopin and Beethoven on the piano."

Carly's father was an incredibly talented pianist. She always felt that if her father hadn't gone into business, he would have been a successful concert pianist.

The Simon children really admired their famous father. They heard stories of how he launched the Simon and Schuster Company in 1923 with a successful crossword puzzle book. Family friend, Bennett Cerf, a publisher himself, said that Richard Simon was a great publisher though he rarely read a book. Apparently Simon had an uncanny instinct for what would sell, a flair for spotting talent, and a way of goading writers into doing their very best.

Richard Simon had other interests besides publishing and the piano. He was known as a superb photographer, a keen bridge and tennis player, and a charmer of women.

Carly found her father to be a king-like, aristocratic figure. She says that her father always felt that he was a very special person and that his children were also terribly special. His faults — such as never allowing himself to be contradicted — along with his strengths made him a dynamic and powerful influence in the lives of all the Simons.

Mr. Simon's talent at the piano often got in the way of Carly's piano playing. Whenever she practiced, her father would say, "No, darling, play it like this." Carly would get up, her father would sit down at the piano and play for hours, completely forgetting that Carly had been practicing. Soon Carly lost interest and stopped taking lessons after about a year when she was 8 or 9.

Carly recalls that she was an overly sensitive child and stammered as she spoke. Her mother, Andrea Simon, who still lives on the family estate in Riverdale, New York, encouraged Carly to express herself in song. Carly gained much confidence from her mother's encouragement. The stammer was soon gone.

Carly and her mother remain close. Audiences have become familiar with a middle-aged woman who pounds on the table and cries for more at Carly's nightclub performances. Mrs. Simon is Carly's biggest fan.

When the Simon children were growing up, they spent a great deal of time at their country home in Martha's Vineyard. Lasting friendships were made there, especially with the neighboring James Taylor family. The Simon children and their friends used to put on plays and musicals in a little theater they had in the barn. Peter was the only Simon with no interest in music. He was always taking pictures somewhere on the island.

Mr. Simon would often bring friends home to watch his children's performances. Carly recalls that their audiences were filled with "heavy people" although at the time she didn't know how important they were. Richard Rodgers and Oscar Hammerstein, famous Broadway musical writers, used to watch them do their song-and-dance routines. Artur Rubinstein, classical pianist, would sit and listen to Mr. Simon play the piano.

Richard Simon's brothers were also prominent in the music world. Alfred Simon was a consultant and writer on theater music and director of light music at a radio

station for 25 years. George Simon played drums in the Glenn Miller Orchestra and is now executive director of the National Academy of Recording Arts and Sciences. Henry Simon, the fourth brother, was music editor for Simon and Schuster.

Carly feels that the musical atmosphere in which she grew up was one of the biggest factors in her decision to become a singer and composer.

Music wasn't the only interest Carly had while growing up. When she was 10, Carly kept a scrapbook on the Brooklyn Dodgers and said she lived for baseball. "Nothing else interested me," Carly once said. "My friends barely did. It was the Dodgers and my father." Carly has often told interviewers that her relationship with her father was very important to her as she was growing up.

Carly had a very easy relationship with her oldest sister Joanna. Because Joanna was 6 years older than Carly, the two never had to compete. Carly enjoyed her brother Peter. But Lucy, only 3 years older, was someone Carly wanted to copy.

Carly followed Lucy through the Riverdale Country School for Girls. Like Lucy, Carly was a cheerleader and tried hard to be popular.

Carly can remember every detail of Lucy's life during high school. She wore the same clothes as Lucy, and she wore her hair in the same style. "For a number of years," Carly says, "I was Lucy."

In her *Hotcakes* album Carly sings about her "Older Sister." The song lists the ways in which Carly imitated Lucy. The refrain contains her high school wish: "Oh, but to be; oh, but to be; oh, but to be; I'd like to be my older sister."

Even when Lucy went away from home after high school, Carly still imitated her. Lucy became a beatnik with pierced ears and frazzle-edged jeans. Carly copied the style and started a whole new trend at the Riverdale School. Carly seemed to be an innovator, but she knew she was still only copying Lucy.

When Lucy went to nursing school, the imitating stopped. Carly could not see herself as a nurse. It was a time when Carly grew fonder of Lucy and a time when Carly felt freer to be her own self, too. At that point Lucy and Carly started singing together.

It became a time for new experiences. Still the old experiences were not gone. Carly would keep looking back on her days at school, her summers at Martha's Vineyard, her relationships with her family and friends, and in them find material for songs.

Carly has kept her fascination with time. What happened yesterday and what will happen tomorrow are questions she asks over and over in her songs.

"What do the people at the end of the world do about time?
What about time?
Their secret sleeps with me."

"The Best Thing"

In the early 1960's Joanna was becoming an opera singer, and Lucy and Carly were harmonizing as folk singers. In 1963 Carly dropped out of Sarah Lawrence College to do more singing with her sister. They performed regularly at the Bitter End, a coffeehouse in New York.

The Simon Sisters, as they were called, also began recording. Lucy and Carly set nursery rhymes to music and made their debut with the Columbia album, *The Simon Sisters Sing the Lobster Quadrille and Other Poems for Children.*

The Simon Sisters' harmony and expression continued to improve in the 2 albums they made for Kapp Records: *Winkin' Blinkin' and Nod / The Simon Sisters* and *The Simon Sisters / Cuddlebug.*

In these albums Lucy and Carly often took traditional songs and made them unique through their own expression and point of view. Lucy and Carly translated the famous Dylan ballad, "Blowin' in the Wind," into French and sang it with a slight rock feel. "Dink's Blues," a song composed and sung by Carly alone, reveals the beginnings of the Carly Simon sound known today.

That's The Way I've Heard It Should Be

15

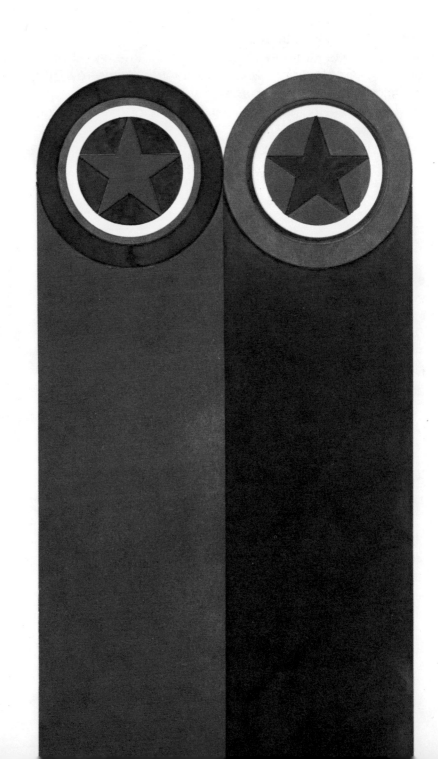

It was difficult, though, to be a folk singer at that time. Folk singers were always compared with Joan Baez, the Queen of Folk. That pressure, along with Lucy's decision to get married, brought an end to the Simon Sisters' musical team.

After Lucy got married, Carly stopped singing and performing. She ran into some problems with a rock manager who wanted to sell her music with the label, "The Female Dylan." Carly felt she was being used because the manager never listened to her. He didn't see that Carly disliked being molded to fit an image.

It was a difficult time for Carly. Again she felt as though she were the loser in the family. Joanna was well-established as an opera singer by that time. Lucy was happily married to a doctor. Peter seemed successful in his free-lance photography work.

Carly spent a few years doing jobs that held no challenge or interest for her. She worked as a secretary, she wrote jingles for commercials, and for a while she taught guitar. No job eased her unsettledness. She wasn't finding what it was that would make her happy.

When Carly looks back on these years, she says, "I think I felt a desire to break away from what my parents felt was important." Carly's rebellious spirit grew as she grew. Because her father was a book publisher, Carly says she tried her hardest never to open a book. "For a long time," Carly once told an interviewer, "I was feeling that the only way I could get anyone's attention or love was by being the black sheep who wasn't making any money, didn't have a job, didn't fit in."

Carly thought she could escape some of her feelings by living for a while in France with a friend. But every night Carly woke up with the shakes. Her friend told her she wasn't shaking, and Carly became convinced that she was crazy. She headed for home and a psychiatrist.

The psychiatrist helped Carly to see that she was too anxious about herself and about life. So Carly spent the next 4 years seeing the psychiatrist regularly. She delved into her past, trying to find out about the things that were bothering her.

Years later after Carly had finished with the psychiatrist, she found the cause of her shaking. One evening while eating at a French restaurant in New York, Carly ordered the same wine she had always had while living in France. That night she began to shake and soon discovered that she was allergic to the wine.

One thing helped Carly through these difficult years. She was able to express her thoughts and feelings in songs. She received much encouragement from Jacob Brackman, a friend and writer. Through the encouragement of both Jake and her brother Peter, Carly began to take her songs seriously.

Another friend, David Bromberg, who respected Carly's talents, helped her to make a demonstration record for Elektra Records. Jac Holzman, then president of Elektra, signed Carly immediately on the basis of the demonstration record and his recollection of the Simon Sisters.

Carly's first single was the break she needed. She and Brackman co-wrote, "That's the Way I've Always Heard It Should Be." That song won her the 1971 Grammy as Best New Artist. It was also the song that put her on the road toward becoming one of the leading singers and songwriters in America.

A reviewer of her first album, *Carly Simon*, said that some of the songs sounded like contemporary short stories set to music. The same reviewer also said that the woman in these songs is both romantic and realistic.

Half of the songs on *Carly Simon* were written several years before the album was recorded. Carly looks back on some of these songs; and, while she still likes them, she feels many are very different from the kind of thing she would write now. But change, Carly feels, is good. She would worry if she didn't see the subject matter changing as she changes.

"Anticipation, anticipation
Is making me late,
Is keeping me waiting."

Anticipation

Fear is a feeling Carly knows well. Two fears in particular have affected her career. After having been silent on the music scene for several years, Carly was

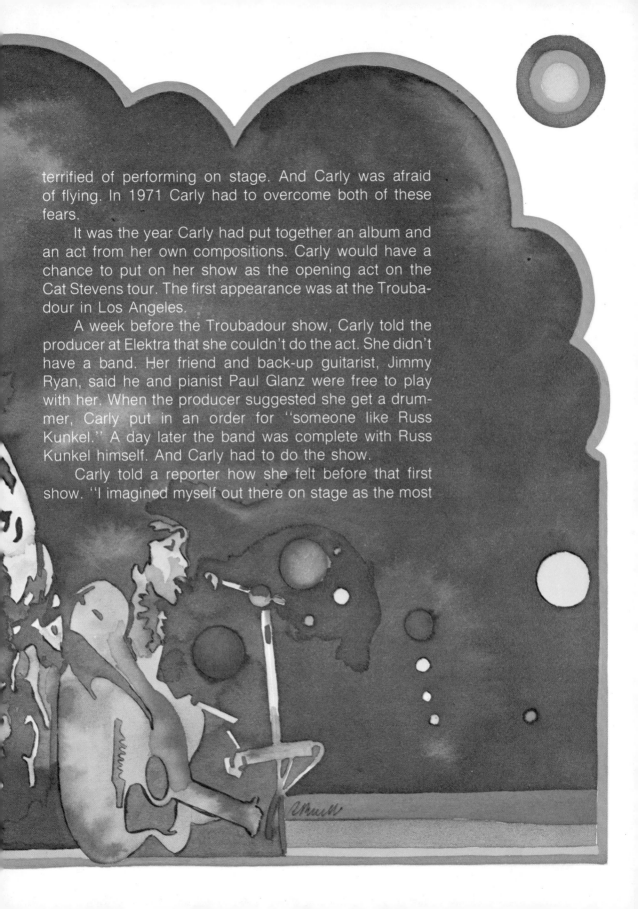

terrified of performing on stage. And Carly was afraid of flying. In 1971 Carly had to overcome both of these fears.

It was the year Carly had put together an album and an act from her own compositions. Carly would have a chance to put on her show as the opening act on the Cat Stevens tour. The first appearance was at the Troubadour in Los Angeles.

A week before the Troubadour show, Carly told the producer at Elektra that she couldn't do the act. She didn't have a band. Her friend and back-up guitarist, Jimmy Ryan, said he and pianist Paul Glanz were free to play with her. When the producer suggested she get a drummer, Carly put in an order for "someone like Russ Kunkel." A day later the band was complete with Russ Kunkel himself. And Carly had to do the show.

Carly told a reporter how she felt before that first show. "I imagined myself out there on stage as the most vulnerable creature in the world . . . I thought I was just going to die on stage.''

Carly feared she would be paralyzed and unable to sing a note. A review of the evening tells the story:

"Around Town"
Carly Simon,
Troubadour, Los Angeles
> *"When somebody at Elektra Records said that Carly Simon was 'a big talent,' he wasn't kidding.... The Amazon-sized Miss Simon (she's got to be almost 6 feet in her sandals) proved in live performance that all those rave reviews of her album weren't paeans to the glories of electronics.''*

by John Weisman
Jazz & Pop, April, 1971

Carly had many problems with the microphones. Still the audience loved her. ''That's the Way I've Always Heard It Should Be'' and ''Dan, My Thing'' were the 2 favorites from her album and her show.

Carly performed 3 concerts with Cat Stevens and became a great fan of his. She learned much from him.

Kris Kristofferson was another influence on Carly just as she was getting started again in 1971. A month after the Troubadour show, Carly appeared with Kris at the Bitter End in New York. To get there, she had to fly.

The plane was like the stage to Carly — the most dangerous place in the world. But she made herself fly, and she made herself perform on stage, not once, but many times. As the year went on, the fears lessened.

Carly Simon
"Live at the Bitter End"

"Carly walked onto the stage and smiled at the audience as if they were old friends. Sitting tall and lovely on a stool, long-skirted and high-booted, she looked as if there were no place in the world she'd rather be at that moment than right there on Bleeker Street....

"...you can see her enjoying the sounds and rhythms of each song; and she sings for her audience, she shares her joy with you....Carly moves with each song, through all its transformations, and the movement, with nothing forced, is beautiful to see....

"As Carly sings the lines in 'The Best Thing,' her voice is very high and quiet, and the words are stretched as if they come from her with considerable pain, an emotional pain which her audience can't help but feel."

by Peter Maloney
Changes, July 15, 1971

Despite her fears, Carly was becoming a very successful performer. Then came a new challenge. Carly was to appear with Cat Stevens at Carnegie Hall. Carly's fear almost completely engulfed her. She didn't think she could bring herself to do it. "All my life I've been a coward at heart," she said. When she thought of performing at the place where all the people she admired had performed, she felt it was crazy for her even to try.

Then Carly began using her imagination. Instead of picturing Carnegie Hall, Carly began to think of performing in some small hall in Albuquerque. It worked. Carly felt that evening at Carnegie was the greatest performance she had ever given.

Carly has always preferred a small club. She says she has to have eye contact as much as possible. "It's

my responsibility," she says, "to turn those rows of faces into joy and happiness." This task is easier for Carly to accomplish in a small club. In a big hall Carly will frequently turn around and look at her drummer or guitarist just to be in contact with another human being.

Carly's voice is smooth, rich, and very flexible. It can be gutsy; it can be high and soft. As she sings, Carly follows the melody line, and her phrasing accentuates her lyrics.

The lyrics or subject matter are often the topic of reviews about Carly's records. She is called the queen of suburban blues or a middle-class singer, because of the experiences she has written about. Whatever the label, Carly's songs are expressions of basic human experiences and feelings. One of Carly's strengths is her ability to sing about something personal and yet give a universal feel to the song.

Anyone can understand what Carly is saying in her song, "Alone," on the *Carly Simon* album. Everyone who has ever been at a family gathering knows what Carly is feeling in her song, "Reunions":

"But no one even comments/Except to say 'Goodbye.'/And I don't know if I'll see you again."

Carly went to London to make her second album, *Anticipation*. The title song sets the mood for most of the album. It is a song about always living just around the corner. It's a song about how difficult it is to live today without always planning tomorrow's activities and conversations.

After *Anticipation* was finished, Carly became tired of what she called a "self-pitying stage." She was tired of how that feeling carried over into her songs. *Anticipation* seemed to her to be about things that never quite happened. Carly was ready to turn a new page, to wipe out the melancholy, and to get into new, more positive subjects.

No Secrets

"You always answer my questions, but they don't always answer my prayers."

"I guess I'm very partial to my friends," Carly once said. Besides her family the most important people to Carly are musicians she has worked with and friends from her past.

James Taylor has influenced Carly in a special way. Carly has said that James has influenced her lyrics, her melodies, her playing — everything. Ever since Carly began seeing James a great deal, she has had difficulty writing songs, she says. It seems to be easier for her to write songs when she is feeling miserable. Her relationship with James brought so much happiness to her that it took Carly a longer time to come up with songs for her third album, *No Secrets*.

James Taylor is often referred to as the new symbol of what is happening in music in the 1970's. Group music is lessening; the individual sound is becoming more popular.

James Taylor's rock sound is bittersweet and soft. Critics often say that Taylor doesn't really sing; he just intones. Yet people like his spare, uninflected voice and his equally spare chording on the guitar.

James has built a home on 27 wooded acres in Martha's Vineyard, and many of his songs seem to reflect the images he sees there by the sea. Like Carly, James reveals his feelings in his songs. He sings of fears, of roads traveled and left untraveled. His first album, *Sweet Baby James*, contains the sad but strong song, "Fire and Rain." *Mudslide Slim and the Blue Horizon*, Taylor's second album, contains his hit version of Carole King's song, "You've Got A Friend."

On November 3, 1972, James began a concert at Radio City Music Hall by announcing that he and Carly had married earlier that evening. Stuart Werbin of *Rolling Stone* did a lengthy interview with Carly and James shortly afterward. They told Werbin what being married meant to them.

Carly was concerned that there be no problems with her continuing in her profession. James said that because they are married, they face these problems and attitudes and try to work them out rather than let the problems chase the two away from each other.

The interviewer noted that many of Carly's and James's songs have religious overtones. James responded by saying that religion starts at home for them. Religion means "relinkage," he says. It means getting back to your roots, to wherever you have come from. He and Carly agree on preserving what is basic in their lives and in their music.

One of Carly's unique qualities is that she expresses feelings which many people don't take time to think about or define for themselves. Movie director Mel Brooks once said to Carly, "That's what your talent is — you say things that are obvious, but nobody else thinks to say them."

Carly's relationship with James has brought difficulties as well as happiness. James had acquired a severe habit of drugs. At the beginning of their relationship, Carly didn't understand the extent of James's use of drugs.

She would feel a wall going up between them, barring communication. As James began to go off drugs, Carly could better understand the impact they had on him. When the interviewer asked Carly whether she ever wanted to try some of the drugs James had been on, Carly emphatically replied, "Never." Seeing what drugs had done to James made Carly have a horror for drugs.

Carly kept wanting to improve her music. She began the recording session for the album, *No Secrets*, feeling pressured to make it good. It had to be better than *Anticipation*.

Carly treated each of the songs she had written for this album as though they were her children. She said that her songs were like children going away to college and meeting different people who influenced them in different ways. Some of the influences Carly liked; other she disliked.

It was frequently difficult for her to work with producer Richard Perry. He often suggested that she go in a direction that was unnatural to her. In the end they would both agree to go back and use the recording as she had done it originally. Yet Carly felt that Perry's perfectionism was helpful. She credits him for the perfect rhythm track they put behind Carly's hit, "You're So Vain."

"You're So Vain" was originally a song called "Bless You, Ben." Carly felt it was too sad and scrapped the lyrics but kept most of the melody. Then she went through her notebook and found a line that had been there for a long time: "You're so vain, you probably think this song is about you."

Everyone wonders whom the song is about. There was even a contest run by a DJ in Los Angeles who had his listeners call in their ballot. Kris Kristofferson was

leading. Mick Jagger of the Rolling Stones had also been suggested. And some have even thought it was James Taylor. Carly flatly rejects James as a candidate, but neither will she tell who it is.

Carly feels the 4 best songs on the *No Secrets* album are "The Right Thing To Do," "You're So Vain," "Robin" and "Embrace Me, You Child." Carly wrote "The Right Thing To Do" specifically for James while she was on a plane from Martha's Vineyard to New York. She wrote the lyrics and melody, and then James helped her polish it.

"Nobody But You," the line from James's song on his album, *Walking Man,* is for Carly. It happens to be her favorite song on his album.

Carly and James often work together on songs. Each respects the distinct talent of the other. At home they see their roles overlapping. Sometimes Carly is involved with her music, and James does the dishes. Sometimes it's the other way around.

On January 7, 1974, Carly and James's daughter, Sarah Marie, was born. During the spring of 1974, the Simon-Taylor family and crew toured the U.S. in their comfortable bus. It was James's tour; but Carly almost always joined him for a finale, singing "Mockingbird" from her album, *Hotcakes.*

Hotcakes is a happy album, revealing a happy Carly Simon. In her song, "Misfit," Carly asks why it is considered hip to be miserable. She suggests that not everyone has to be miserable and feel like a misfit in order to be part of things.

"Grownup" is another questioning song. As a child watches Carly sing, Carly remembers how fearless and self-assured grownups looked to her when she was a child. Now Carly realizes that she has just grown a little taller "and the littles ones call me a grownup."

Hotcakes shows that it's a new and happy time for Carly. She sings:

"Suffering was the only thing made me feel I
  was alive
'Til you showed me how to survive, how to fill
  my heart with love.
I haven't got time for the pain
Not since I've known you."

Carly feels she has reached a point of fulfillment both professionally and personally. She doesn't feel that her marriage has taken independence from her. On the contrary, Carly says, "I have more independence since I've gotten married . . . I'm freer to know myself, which is the most important kind of freedom."

Carly's new-found freedom didn't come overnight. It didn't come because she grew up in a wealthy family. Carly's freedom came from living through and accepting every stage in her life. And at every stage, Carly tried to be honest with herself and with the people she dealt with. In "No Secrets" she sings, "We have no secrets. We tell each other everything . . ." While Carly values such honesty, she also acknowledges how difficult it is: "Sometimes I wish that I never knew some of those secrets of yours." As the reviewer said, Carly is a romantic and a realist.

Singing and composing will probably always be something Carly needs to do. It is still one of her strongest ways of proving to herself that she's not a loser. Applause that says, "Carly Simon, you're all right" will always be music to her ears. The famous Richard Simon would be proud to be Carly's father.

JACKSON FIVE
CARLY SIMON
BOB DYLAN
JOHN DENVER
THE BEATLES
ELVIS PRESLEY
JOHNNY CASH
CHARLEY PRIDE
ARETHA FRANKLIN
ROBERTA FLACK
STEVIE WONDER

Rock'n PopStars